TO CALVARY WITH MARY

For Mary Cruickshank

Anthea Dove

To Calvary with Mary

Accompanying the mother of God
as she accompanies her son on his journey to death

the columba press

First published in 2004 by

𝕮𝕳𝕰 𝕮𝕺𝕷𝖀𝕸𝕭𝕬 𝕻𝕽𝕰𝕾𝕾

55A Spruce Avenue, Stillorgan Industrial Estate,
Blackrock, Co Dublin.

Cover by Bill Bolger
Origination by The Columba Press
Printed in Ireland by Paceprint Ltd, Dublin.

ISBN 1-85607-462-5

Preface

I realise there is a kind of presumption in trying to describe the feelings of the mother of God as she endured the Passion of her son.

How can anyone know how it was for Mary, standing at the foot of the cross?

I do know, like any mother, the sharpness of the pain I feel when one of my children is suffering.

This is my excuse for the attempt I have made here.

The agony in the garden

I wish with all my heart that I could have been there, that he had asked me to come and be with him. But he knew I was tired. He had kissed me goodnight and told me to sleep well.

Of course I didn't sleep well. I knew something was wrong, very wrong. And then, this morning, John came round to tell me what had happened.

Jesus took Peter and James and John down to the Garden of Gethsemane, a beautiful place full of ancient silvery olives, and he asked them to stay awake while he prayed. He was a little distance away from them, but John tried to listen when Jesus was praying aloud. He told me that my son pleaded with God, pleaded with his father, to save him from the suffering that was to come. Then he seemed to gather courage, for he said, 'Not my will, but yours be done.' Oh, my poor boy!

John said he must have fallen asleep then, for the next thing he knew was Jesus shaking them all awake and saying, 'Could you not watch one hour with me?'

'He looked terrible, Mary,' John said, 'his face was pouring with sweat. I am filled with shame and sorrow that I failed to keep watch with him.'

I tried to console John. He is probably the best friend Jesus has, and he means well.

But how I wish I had been in that garden with him.

Jesus is condemned to death

When the Roman Governor condemns him, I scream. I don't remember ever screaming before, certainly not like that, so loud and shrill and uncontrolled, screaming my heart out. Afterwards, I am ashamed. I have always tried to behave with a quiet dignity because I didn't want to let him down. But no-one hears me screaming: everyone round me is shouting 'Crucify him! Crucify him!' Oh, it is so cruel. I can't bear it. He stands there, bruised and battered, wearing that ridiculous garment and with blood trickling down his face from the crown of thorns they have placed on his head to mock him. I try to read the expression on his face but I am too far away and my eyes are blurred with tears.

They lead him away then, one of them pushing him roughly, and I know his terrible journey to Golgotha will start soon. I make up my mind to follow, to stay as close to him as I can. But I know it will be difficult to get near him because of the crowds who will be following too. Most of them will be horrible to him; they will jeer and perhaps throw things at him. How can this be happening? How can anyone hate him, Jesus, my son, who is all goodness, all compassion?

I push my way to the place where I know they will bring him. I walk fast, because I want to see him near me, and most of all because I want him to see me, to know that

I am with him, that I will stay with him all the way. People tread on my feet and jostle me with their elbows but I don't care. I reach the place, I find a piece of ground from which I think I'll be able to see him clearly. I stand still and wait. All at once I seem to see the face, not the face of Jesus, but the one I saw just once before, long ago, the one I remember. It is not real; it's only a dream or a memory. But seeing that old holy face, the gentle expression in those sad eyes, I hear Simeon speaking just as clearly as he did all those years ago when he said, 'A sword shall pierce your soul.'

I was so happy then, with Jesus, my baby, in my arms and dear Joseph beside me, but when he said those words I felt suddenly faint and chill; I knew in that moment that one day his words would come true. And now it has happened: a sword has pierced my soul.

Jesus carries his cross

Here Jesus comes, with soldiers on either side and behind him. All round me people are mocking and jeering, excited by the spectacle. He looks a little better now. He is wearing his own clothes and they have taken off the crown of thorns. But he looks so frail and I think he is frightened – Jesus who was never afraid of anything!

I would give anything in the world to take his place.

Oh, look at that cross – it's so heavy, much too heavy for him! He's a strong and healthy man, at least he was until those brutes got hold of him. I don't want to think what they have done to him. I could see that he could hardly stand up when they first brought him out. And now, the weight of that cross – I'm sure it's too much and he will collapse under it.

It's hard to keep him in my sight. There are just too many people, bigger and stronger and younger than me, pushing and shoving. They seem to enjoy the spectacle of a broken man. How can that be? The noise is deafening and the smell of so many bodies pressed together is overwhelming.

But that's nothing compared to his suffering. If I could just catch his eye, just let him see that I am here, so that he will know that he is not quite alone. What I'd really like to do is touch him, hold him, speak to him. But I know that's impossible. And I can't see any of his friends. Surely some of them must be here somewhere?

Jesus falls the first time

Jesus has fallen! I knew he would. That cross is far too heavy. He is lying on the ground and I can't see his face. I try to call his name but my voice is drowned by the noise all around me.

Now he's trying to get up. He's rubbing the sweat out of his eyes and he's actually smiling a little as though he's embarrassed.

Suddenly I remember the first time he fell. He was two years old, running down the hillside to meet Joseph on his way home from work. He stumbled on a stone and fell with a thud. How he yelled! Joseph ran up the hill and I ran down. I remember I was crying myself. Joseph got there first and picked him up, but he handed him to me as soon as I reached them. I held him close and stroked him, but he kept on sobbing. Joseph said, 'Come on, now, little man, you must be brave.' But I was angry and said, 'He's not a man, he's a little boy, and he's hurt!'

Now he is a man and I can't hold him and comfort him.

I can only stand here, so helpless and useless.

Simon of Cyrene

It is such struggle for him to get to his feet. What can they have done to him to make every movement so painful? I can see how he is hurting. I feel the pain in my own body.

But the soldiers don't care. I saw one of them kick him. They are impatient to get this all over, I suppose.

Now one of them has dragged a big black man out of the crowd. He looks bewildered and frightened too.

But this is good! The soldiers are making him help to carry the cross. That's a great relief, for me, and more importantly, it must be for Jesus.

I can't see Jesus' face. I wonder if they will speak to each other? I feel it is a kind of blessing on this stranger to be carrying the cross, even if he doesn't know it. And it helps me too, to see my son no longer so completely abandoned.

Jesus falls a second time

Jesus has fallen again. I think he stumbled on a stone, but this time he fell flat on his face, and he is not moving. For a second the thought, the wish, flashes through me: it would be better for him to die, right there on the ground where he is, rather than have to face what is to come. But of course my will for him to live, if only for a few more hours, is stronger, and as long as he is alive I can hold on to the hope that a miracle will deliver him from all this. The big man is bending down and helping him to his feet again.

The first time Jesus fell, he looked embarrassed, but now I can see he doesn't care any more about the shame of falling. I think he is in a lot of pain and his poor face looks dreadful, covered in blood and mud and sweat – and, I think, tears. If only I could reach him and gently wipe all that away.

The women of Jerusalem

Another woman is doing what I longed to do. I wish it could have been me, but of course it doesn't really matter, as long as someone can give him comfort and relief. The woman is wearing beautiful clothes, she looks elegant and fastidious and it's hard to imagine why she is here among all these rough and noisy people.

But now I see there are others with her, the same kind of women, and the soldiers, who have no respect for my son, the son of God, treat these ladies with respect. Looking at them, I remember being told once that the noble women of Jerusalem take on the responsibility of comforting criminals. It is so good of them and I feel touched that they are actually weeping for Jesus, just as I am weeping.

But he is speaking! I strain to hear what he is saying. His voice is faint and there is so much noise all round me, but I can just hear these words: 'Daughters of Jerusalem, do not weep for me; weep rather for yourselves and for your children.'

I am not surprised. He has never shown self-pity, and always more concern for others than for himself.

I am so grateful to these women. I wish I could get near them to thank them, but the crowd is surging on and carrying me with it.

Jesus falls the third time

He has fallen again! It is too much to bear!

His wounds and sores will be opened again after hitting the ground, and from the way he is lying I can see that he is utterly exhausted.

There are too many people barring my way. I cannot get near to him, I can only stand on tiptoe and peer between the shoulders of strangers. He lies quite still on the ground where he has fallen. It is as though he is already dead.

The soldiers are angry. One of them kicks Jesus viciously; another gives the big man a hard shove so that he almost falls over too. But he steadies himself and bends down, saying something to Jesus who is still motionless on the ground.

Very gently, this time, the big man pulls him to his feet. When I see Jesus' face I cry out, and some people nearby turn briefly to stare at me, but they are not interested in me, only in the spectacle of a bruised and battered man on his way to death.

Jesus is stripped

I have felt many emotions already today: deep sadness, great love, frustration and outrage. Now I begin to feel afraid, not for myself but for my son.

We are nearly there. The soldiers have seized the cross from him and laid it on the ground, near two others.

I see now that there are two other men, two poor wretches, held roughly by soldiers and waiting for the same dreadful fate. I feel a pang of pity for them, but when I turn and look at Jesus again, I forget the other two, because they are tearing off my son's clothes. Must he bear this indignity on top of everything else?

Suddenly there is a lot more jeering and mocking, laughter even. I have to hold myself still to prevent myself from striking out at one of those cruel faces. I don't do it because I know it would be of no help to him, and if the soldiers seized me too it would only increase his distress.

His body is thin and pale; his back is streaked with bloody stripes from the lash. And he is shivering, in spite of the heat from bodies all around him. How I long to wrap him in my cloak and hold him close.

I care so much because he is my son, and because I know he is perfectly innocent and good. But when I look at him, I think also of all those like him, the world's suffering people. I think of those who are poor, oppressed, afraid, hungry or friendless.

Jesus is nailed to the cross

Oh, my God! I cannot bear to look. Suddenly the crowd is silent. The soldiers have laid him flat on the cross with his arms outstretched and they are about to pierce his hands and feet with nails, to fix him to the wood. This is too much for me. I close my eyes as the hammer thuds on the nails. But when he cries out in agony my eyes fly open and I rush forward. Strong hands hold me back.

Now one of the soldiers, kneeling by Jesus' right hand and holding the hammer ready to strike (he has already nailed his left hand to the crossbar), is actually laughing and joking with the crowd.

But not all of the crowd are enjoying this. Some of them have turned away or closed their eyes like I did. An old man near me muttered 'Shame!' and I managed to smile at him. I am grateful for any pity or kindness shown to my son.

I force myself to look at him again. He is there, helpless and clearly in terrible pain. His hands and feet are bleeding.

And then, strangely, from somewhere, I feel I have been given a great strength. I have stopped weeping now and I am very calm, ready to face whatever happens.

The good thief

I watch the men hoisting the heavy crosses and steadying them with ropes so that they stand upright in the ground.

Some of the chief priests and scribes and elders are still here. I would not have believed they could be so cruel. They are as bad as some of the passers-by who taunt Jesus and jeer at him. I hear one of them shouting above the others: 'He saved others,' he mocks, 'let him save himself. He is the King of Israel; let him come down from the cross now, and we will believe in him.'

One of the robbers on the cross next to him is taunting him too, but the other speaks up. 'Have you no fear of God at all?' he says. 'You got the same sentence as he did, but in our case we deserved it. We are paying for what we did. But this man has done nothing wrong.' Then he turns to Jesus and says, 'Please remember me when you come into your kingdom.'

Jesus answers: 'Today you will be with me in paradise.'

Most of the people shuffle away. Some are afraid, some indifferent. There is plenty of space now; at last. I walk forward and stand by his cross, so near that I can touch the wood.

I realise that I am not alone. Others have come to be near him in this last hour of dreadful suffering, perhaps, some of them, to support me too. I see that my dear sister is with me and Mary, the wife of Clopas and Mary of

Magdala. But apart from the soldiers, there is only one man, John.

Mary and John

We all look up at Jesus. I see that apart from the pain, he has great difficulty in breathing. Oh, if only he can die quickly now!

It has gone dark, and cold too. My strength is failing again. I can't take in everything that's happening. I can't even hear everything that Jesus is trying to say. It's such a struggle for him to speak.

There is one moment I will particularly remember for always. Jesus looks down and sees me. I have been waiting for this all day. I try to smile, try to look reassuring and strong. But he sees through me, just as he always does. Even in the midst of his agony, he understands my need.

He cannot smile; he can hardly breathe. Still he struggles to speak. He looks at John, and then again at me, and we both strain to hear his words.

To me he says: 'Woman, behold your son', and to John, 'This is your mother.' John puts an arm round me and I lean against his shoulder. I know then that he will look after me and take me to live in his home, and I am grateful. John is a dear man, but there is simply no comparison between him and Jesus. He could never take the place of my son.

Jesus dies

We stand here, bewildered, powerless, desperately sad. We hang on every word that comes from the lips of Jesus, but it is difficult to take it all in. Do I stand there for a very long time, or is it all over in a flash? I shall never know.

I hear the hoarse cry, 'I am thirsty', and I see someone run to soak a sponge in the rough wine the soldiers drink. He puts it on the end of a reed and lifts it to Jesus' mouth. But then I see that his mouth doesn't move and his eyes are staring and I know that he is dead.

I wish, how I wish, that I could die too.

Jesus is buried

I am cradling him in my arms. In some ways it's like when he was first born, so small and fragile, completely dependent on me. But then he was beautiful, perfect. Now he is ugly and broken, bruised and bleeding, as it is written 'a thing despised and rejected of men'.

I bend to kiss his poor dear face; it is still warm. I am sitting on the ground beneath that terrible cross and I begin to rock to and fro. My tears fall freely, softly, copiously over his face and body, washing away at least some of the dirt and blood. I think, shall I sing a lullaby? But my voice won't work. I wonder, am I going mad?

Then they come, the good men, the strong men, Joseph of Arimathea and John, and they gently lift the body of Jesus and carry him over to a bier. Next Nicodemus comes, bringing aloes and myrrh, with their clean sweet fragrance. My women friends lift me to my feet and I watch while they wash him and wrap him with the spices in a white linen cloth.

It is only a short way to the garden, where Joseph shows us a new burial place cut into the rock. They lay Jesus there, and then they all wait patiently while I, dry-eyed now, look on him in silence. When I give Joseph the signal, they take a great boulder and place it across the entrance to the tomb.

They lead me away. I feel nothing.

The resurrection

I am in John's house. He has gone to join James and Peter and the others. He said he would leave me to sleep.

But I cannot sleep. I haven't slept since Jesus died – when? Was it yesterday, two days ago? Time has no meaning for me any more.

When they buried him, I felt nothing, but now I am overwhelmed with feelings: with anguish and despair, with terrible anger and searing pity.

I am trying to clear my mind, trying to remember every detail of those last hours of my son's life. He tried to speak, over and over, but it was so hard for him to get the words out. I recall the shock I felt when I heard him say: 'My God, my God, why hast thou forsaken me?' Could he have given up all hope in the Father he loved so deeply? Did he feel so completely abandoned? Surely not.

And then, who but Jesus could have shown such mercy to his torturers and murderers? But I did distinctly hear him say, 'Father, forgive them, for they know not what they do.' It will take me much, much longer, my whole life, perhaps, to forgive them.

It is a consolation, a small one, to me now, that his very last words revealed that his trust in his Father's love was after all secure. 'Father,' he said, 'into your hands I commit my spirit.'

I still wish I could die. My body is utterly exhausted. I have not eaten or slept for days, but I am alive.

Mary of Magdala came round this morning, very early, when it was still dark. She said she was going to the tomb and invited me to go with her.

I said nothing. She lit the lamp and came closer to me. 'I can see you are worn out, Mary,' she said then, 'it is better that you rest. Try to eat something and get some sleep. Perhaps you will come to the tomb tomorrow.'

I looked up at her gratefully. Her face was pale and stained with tears. She bent to kiss me and then she left.

I try to do as Mary said, but it's no use. I can't make myself either eat or sleep. After a while I see the sky is lightening so I blow out the lamp. I go out of the house and I see Mary of Magdala running up the hill towards me. The sun is rising behind her and at first I can't see her face clearly, but as she comes close I can see that her eyes are shining.

Mary of Magdala calls my name and stretches out her arms to me. Her smile is brighter than the sunrise.